RUTHERFORD B. HAYES

ENCYCLOPEDIA
of PRESIDENTS

Rutherford B. Hayes

Nineteenth President of the United States

By Zachary Kent

Consultant: Charles Abele, Ph.D.
Social Studies Instructor
Chicago Public School System

CHILDRENS PRESS ®
CHICAGO

Rutherford B. Hayes
speaking to a crowd
in Louisville, Kentucky,
in 1877

Library of Congress Cataloging-in-Publication Data

Kent, Zachary.
   Rutherford B. Hayes.

   (Encyclopedia of presidents)
   Includes index.
   Summary: Examines the life and career of
the Civil War general and Ohio politician
who became the nineteenth president of the
United States.
   1. Hayes, Rutherford Birchard, 1822-1893
—Juvenile literature.   2.   Presidents—United
States—Biography—Juvenile literature.
3.   United States—Politics and government
—1877-1881—Juvenile literature.   [1.   Hayes,
Rutherford Birchard, 1822-1893.   2.   Presidents]
I.   Title.   II.   Series.
E682.K28   1989 · 973.8'3'0924   [B]   [92]   88-8679
ISBN 0-516-01365-3

Picture Acknowledgments

The Granger Collection—36 (2 pictures), 45, 48,
53 (top), 57 (bottom), 59, 63, 64 (top), 78, 84
(top), 88

Historical Pictures Service, Chicago—12, 14, 19,
30, 44, 51, 53 (bottom), 58, 61, 71, 73 (2
pictures), 76, 77, 79

Library of Congress—66, 67

North Wind Picture Archives—28, 29, 82

Ohio State University Archives—43

Rutherford B. Hayes Presidential Center, Spiegel
Grove, Fremont, Ohio—4, 5, 6, 8, 10, 16, 17, 20,
22, 24, 25, 26, 31, 33, 34, 35, 38, 40, 41, 42, 47
(2 pictures), 57 (top), 62, 64 (bottom), 65 (2
pictures), 68, 75, 80, 84 (bottom), 87, 89

U.S. Bureau of Printing and Engraving—2

Cover design and illustration
by Steven Gaston Dobson

Lucy and Rutherford Hayes, friend W. H. Smith, and Dot the dog at Spiegel Grove

Table of Contents

Chapter 1

The Good Colonel

Union soldiers of the Twenty-Third Ohio Infantry Regiment scattered across the wooded field. Officers galloped on horseback shouting orders, while enlisted men hurriedly unfurled flags and loaded muskets. The American Civil War had been raging for more than a year. In that time these veteran Ohio volunteers had learned how to form a battle line with expert skill. Before them on a steep hill, the Confederate enemy crouched behind rocks and trees. On September 14, 1862, the gray-clad rebels guarded a pass called Fox's Gap at South Mountain, Maryland, and the Union army was determined to smash through.

Along the Union battle line, a bearded thirty-nine-year-old lieutenant colonel rode. The men of the Twenty-Third Ohio loudly cheered as they recognized their beloved commander, Rutherford B. Hayes. Trooper E. E. Henry later exclaimed, "Lieutenant Colonel Hayes is a lion of a leader. . . . We see Colonel Hayes come riding at a gallop the whole length of the line, waving his sword, the grand anger of battle flashing in his eyes. . . . It puts fight in us to see Colonel Hayes riding at full gallop. . . . *Who could not follow him in battle . . . ?*"

Hayes at Red Bud Creek in the Battle of Opequon, Virginia

"Now, boys, remember you are the 23rd, and give them Hell," Hayes shouted, as he ordered his men to charge. Spurring his horse, he started up the hill, and with a yell his soldiers plunged after him. "Give them Hell!" cried Hayes again. Cannon boomed and musket volleys sent bullets whizzing through the air. Wounded Yankees and rebels screamed and fell across the wooded slope. Later Hayes declared, "Our men halted at a fence and kept up a brisk fire upon the enemy, who were sheltering themselves behind stone walls and fences near the top of the hill beyond a cornfield in front of our position."

Sensing victory, Hayes dismounted and called for his troops to charge again. Just then the stunning blow of a musket ball struck his left arm above the elbow. The bullet ripped away skin and flesh, cracked the bone, and tore an artery. As blood poured from the wound, Hayes dropped to the ground feeling faint and sick. Wisely he called upon a soldier to twist a handkerchief around his arm to stop the heavy bleeding. Forcing himself to his feet he urged his men to hold their positions and keep fighting. "I am played out," an exhausted sergeant begged. "Please, sir, let me leave." With his sword, Hayes pointed at his helpless, bloodied arm. "Look at this," he exclaimed. "Don't talk about being played out. There is your place in line."

As the battle raged, Hayes sank faintly to the ground again. "Balls passed near my face and hit the ground all around me," he marveled. The colonel rested, though he sometimes shouted directions to his troops. On the ground nearby lay a wounded Confederate soldier. "You came a long way to fight us," Hayes remarked. The Confederate asked where he was from and Hayes answered, "I am from Ohio." "Well," the injured rebel countered, "you came a good ways to fight us."

Flat on his back Hayes lay sprawled as musket balls whistled all around him. Then he noticed a lull in the fighting. Looking about he saw that the Union troops were shifting away from the field. With the last of his strength Hayes desperately called out, "Hello, Twenty-third men! Are you going to leave your colonel here for the enemy?" At the sound of his voice, half a dozen men rushed back to rescue him. They carried him behind the lines to safety.

The Twenty-Third Ohio Infantry in the Battle of South Mountain, Maryland

At a field hospital a surgeon dressed Hayes's wound. His arm hanging limply, the colonel stumbled another half mile to an ambulance. The simple wagon bounced over the road to nearby Middletown, Maryland. There Hayes was given a room in a local home. One hundred thirty of his men had suffered bloody wounds or death that day. The colonel learned with satisfaction, though, that the Union had won the battle. The mountain pass was captured.

Luckily for Hayes, his brother-in-law, Joseph Webb, served as regimental surgeon of the Twenty-Third Ohio. That evening Doctor Webb arrived in Middletown to take care of Hayes himself. In crude and crowded hospital tents, doctors usually sawed off badly mangled arms and legs in the jumbled aftermath of battle. Doctor Webb, however, was determined to give his brother-in-law the best possible treatment.

In Ohio, Lucy Hayes soon received a message from her wounded husband: "I am here, come to me. I shall not lose my arm." Anxiously she hurried east, and with difficulty she found her husband. Through the next weeks she performed the duties of a loving nurse, changing his bandages and keeping his broken arm carefully splinted. A strong will and kind attention led to the injured man's speedy recovery. In November 1862 members of the Twenty-Third Ohio yelled greetings as Hayes returned to camp.

Although a gentleman lawyer at the outbreak of the Civil War, Rutherford B. Hayes promptly joined the Northern cause. Through four years of hard warfare, his warm, modest nature and fierce fighting spirit endeared him to his troops.

After the war Hayes honorably pursued a successful political career. As a result, in 1876 the Republican party selected him to run for nineteenth United States president. The election of that year would be the most disputed in American history, but after much argument Hayes finally took office. Through the next four troubled years he steered the nation with dignity and purpose.

Even as an old man, however, Hayes's army service remained his proudest accomplishment. "I am more gratified by friendly references to my war record," he remarked in his later years, "than by any other flattery." And he added, "I know that my place was a very humble one—a place utterly unknown in history. But I also am glad to know that I was one of the good colonels." In the end, his lasting concern for Union comrades and beaten Confederate foes made Hayes a well-respected president.

Chapter 2

The Education of a Gentleman

In the darkness of October 4, 1822, Sardis Birchard sprang from the steps of the Hayes family home on William Street in Delaware, Ohio. He hurried along the road to get medical help for his pregnant sister, Sophia Birchard Hayes. "It was a gloomy night," he later recalled. "I went for Dr. Lamb. . . . It was rather cool for the season. I built a fire. Mrs. Smith, a most excellent nurse, attended. . . ." Soon an infant's cries revealed the birth of Rutherford Birchard Hayes. "I paid Dr. Lamb $3.50 for his job," commented the baby's Uncle Sardis.

It was a time of mourning in the Hayes family. The baby's father, Rutherford Hayes, had carted his wife and children westward from Vermont in 1817. In Ohio, Hayes grew into a successful merchant and landowner. Young Rutherford later declared: "My father was straight, slender, healthy and active, full of energy and life—a witty, social, popular man who made warm friends and few enemies." Sadly, while clearing a field in July 1822, a fever struck down Rutherford Hayes, and three days later he died. Two-and-a-half months after his burial, his wife, Sophia, gave birth to his last son and namesake.

Hayes's birthplace in Delaware, Ohio

In the fatherless house, the baby, called "Ruddy," struggled to survive his infancy. One neighbor gazed at his weak body, born thin and sickly, and sighed, "It would be a mercy if the child would die." Sophia Hayes remembered, "For two years I had little hope of his life." With loving care, however, she nursed her son along.

Grief shook the Hayes family again in January 1825. Ruddy's nine-year-old brother, Lorenzo, went skating on a frozen pond. Suddenly the thin ice cracked and the boy plunged through and drowned. The tragic death of Lorenzo made Sophia Hayes more protective than ever of her only remaining son. As he grew older and sturdier Ruddy endured his mother's constant, smothering attention. She heaped food upon his plate at mealtimes and spoiled him with candy. Later she admitted she "kept him in the house a good deal." In fact, during his early years, Ruddy was not allowed to play outside. His protective mother refused when he offered to do simple household chores, and rather than let him attend school, she herself taught him to read, write, and spell.

As a result of his loneliness Ruddy grew extremely close to his sister, Fanny, who was two years older. A bright and lovely girl, Fanny told him stories and thought of games to play. Together they raced across the hallway carpet and played hide-and-seek behind the draperies in the comfortable Hayes home. "The confidante of all my life," he called her. As constant companions, the two kept no secrets from each other. Fanny's sense of independence and high spirits deeply affected her brother. "Oh, her beautiful character, her winning ways . . . her sweet affections!" he later recalled. "She loved me as an only sister loves a brother whom she imagines almost perfect, and I loved her as an only brother loves a sister who is perfect."

As Ruddy stretched in size, frequent visits by wealthy bachelor Uncle Sardis Birchard brought a manly influence into the Hayes house. "My children are perfectly well," Sophia Hayes told a friend one day, "but I am filled with fear for them." With her brother Sardis's encouragement, Sophia Hayes gradually became less anxious about her healthy son. After the age of seven he was allowed outside more often. During visits to the family's farm outside of town, Ruddy enjoyed running and shouting in the fields. In the autumns he helped the farm's workers press apples into cider.

Sophia Birchard Hayes

Clearly happy out-of-doors, Ruddy was given plenty of freedom. "Rud! Rud! Look out for the mud!" youthful friends teased him. At the age of nine Ruddy joined in playing sports and enjoyed fishing, swimming, and skating. Stalking squirrels in the woods, he showed himself a crack marksman. On the baseball field he hurled the ball with skill. The local boys were pleased and proud to have Ruddy Hayes for a comrade.

Fanny remained Ruddy's closest companion. Indoors they performed little plays, painted together, and invented tricks. Outside, Fanny often shocked straightlaced neighbors by acting like a tomboy. "She was the best rifle shot of any lady I ever knew," exclaimed Ruddy. "She could even beat Uncle Sardis in playing chess and shooting a rifle at a mark." Fanny later wrote to her brother: "As I recall our early days, they were all long merry ones, when we laughed & laughed, if it were only at the sound of each

Uncle Sardis Birchard

other's voices. Those weekly walks to the farm are only
remembered as rambles in the shade when, sitting down,
we bathed our feet in the brook & watched the minnows,
or gathered pebbles." Fanny mothered Ruddy through his
youth, urging him to become "somebody important."

Self-assured and intelligent, Ruddy sometimes impressed listeners by reciting famous patriotic speeches he
had memorized. While attending private school in town he
proved himself an outstanding scholar and a champion
speller. "Not one in a thousand could spell me down!" he
once bragged. He much preferred outdoor work to school,
however. Gladly he painted the house, dug a well, and performed other strenuous chores. "Rutherford is a good
boy," explained Sophia Hayes, but "he should be at some-
thing of more importance." She agreed with Uncle Sardis
that her son should attend a private academy and acquire
the knowledge of a young gentleman.

In the fall of 1836, fourteen-year-old Rutherford entered Norwalk Academy in Norwalk, Ohio. Although sometimes homesick, he excitedly made new friends. "I am doing very well in my studies," he wrote to his mother. "Wednesday was composition day. I wrote one about Liberty. A week ago Wednesday was speaking day. . . . I got along tolerably well, considering. I was not scared, as much as the most of the boys are the first time they speak." During the following school year Rutherford attended classes at Isaac Webb's Preparatory School in Middletown, Connecticut. Easily he kept up with his fellow students, winning prizes in Latin and Greek. For fun he joined a secret school club called the Cobwebs.

When the time came, Rutherford's mother and uncle carefully chose the college he should attend. Kenyon College was a fine school, located not far from Delaware in Gambier, Ohio. In the fall of 1838 sixteen-year-old Hayes enrolled there. His friendliness and enthusiasm made him instantly popular with the other students. One classmate, Lorin Andrews, remembered Hayes as a "first-rate fellow." Mischievously, Rutherford sometimes defied school regulations and went hunting with his comrades. "We were forbidden to have any guns," he later fondly recalled. "I always had two. There were also strict rules against cooking in the rooms, but we cooked and I had considerable of a reputation as a cook. . . ." Friends cheered when Hayes batted in baseball games or crossed the finish line first in races. Sometimes northern students angrily argued with southern students about the cruelty of black slavery in the South. Often it was Hayes's even temper

Kenyon College in Gambier, Ohio

that smoothed the matter over and stopped fights. Everyone liked and respected Rutherford Hayes.

He made his mark in the classroom, too. "Do not waste your time in school as so many do," his mother warned him. "*Be a good boy. Be first in your class,*" his sister lovingly prodded. With determination Hayes set out to fulfill their wishes, swearing "to use what means I have to acquire a character distinguished for energy, firmness, and perseverance." Through hard work he earned top grades in his studies and proved an expert debater.

In his senior year the college reported: "For strength of mind, clearness of perception, [and] soundness of judgment, he is surpassed by none among us. In all his studies, he has attained the highest grade. . . . His conduct has been most gentlemanly. . . ." Finishing at the head of his class, Hayes delivered a fine valedictory address during the August 1842 graduation ceremony.

Hayes (left) and two friends at Kenyon College

Hayes departed Kenyon College feeling "much as if a load were off my stomach." His sister had married William Platt of Columbus, Ohio, and Hayes moved in with them for a time. Having chosen the law for his future profession, he entered the Columbus law office of Thomas Sparrow to work and study. Hayes threw himself into the effort. In his diary on November 26, 1842, he scribbled, "My rules for the month are: First, Read no newspapers. Second, Rise at seven and retire at ten. Third, Study law six hours. . . ."

Soon he recognized the value of more formal legal study and decided to enter Harvard Law School. Proudly Sardis Birchard agreed to pay his nephew's tuition costs. "The money will be well paid out," he remarked. "Rutherford is a sound boy and has got good hard sense, like a Horse." At the age of twenty-one Hayes traveled to Cambridge, Massachusetts, to embark upon two more years of careful classwork. In January 1845, he at last obtained his law degree. "Now I shall begin to *live!*" he declared as he journeyed back to Ohio.

To show his independence from his mother and sister, Hayes chose to practice law in the little town of Lower Sandusky, Ohio, where his Uncle Sardis lived. In partnership with another lawyer, Ralph Buckland, Hayes opened a small office.

"Buckland & Hayes Attorneys at Law. Will attend to the Business of Their Profession in Sandusky and Adjoining counties," a local newspaper soon advertised. Unfortunately, business remained slow in sleepy Lower Sandusky during Hayes's five years there. To his mother he teased, "I have hopes of living to see the place at least half-civilized one of these afternoons." Truthfully, though, he felt deeply frustrated. "Oh, the waste of those five precious years!" he later exclaimed.

In May 1846 a territorial war erupted between the United States and Mexico. For a time Hayes excitedly hoped to march south and join the fight. His mother sighed with relief when doctors advised against it. The stress Hayes suffered from his business, as well as bouts of tonsillitus, kept him out of the Mexican War.

Hayes studying law in his room in Columbus, Ohio

Hayes took an active role in local affairs. When the town council decided to rename Lower Sandusky, Hayes headed the commission that would make the choice. In the end they picked the name Fremont, to honor American explorer John C. Frémont.

In time Hayes realized he must move if he wished to become a successful lawyer. To the south in the city of Cincinnati scores of steamboats crowded the Ohio River landings and busy people thronged the streets. On Christmas Day in 1849, twenty-seven-year-old Rutherford B. Hayes arrived there in search of fresh opportunities.

Sharing an office with another struggling lawyer named John W. Herron, Hayes soon commented, "We sleep on little hard mattresses in a little room cooped off from one end of our office." Hayes's new motto became "Push, Labor, Shove." To his uncle he confided, "All who stay and are found in their offices ready to do business, do get it." To attract additional clients, Hayes joined local social clubs and gave lectures on public issues. In time, his reputation as both a speaker and a lawyer grew.

Standing five feet nine inches tall, Hayes cut a handsome figure as he walked the streets of Cincinnati. His blue eyes, brown hair, and fine, straight features touched the heart of more than one young lady. For a time Hayes courted Miss Fanny Perkins, a charming Connecticut girl who was visiting in Ohio. He even proposed marriage to her. The couple quarreled, however, when she insisted that they live in Connecticut. Stubbornly, he broke off their relationship.

For several years Hayes had shown an interest in a young woman named Lucy Webb. The daughter of a doctor who had died when she was a baby, Lucy lived with her widowed mother in Delaware, Ohio. While Lucy attended the Wesleyan Woman's College in Cincinnati, Hayes escorted her to parties and dances. In time the young lawyer revealed in his diary: "Her low sweet voice is very winning, her soft rich eyes not often equalled, a heart as true as steel, I know. . . . Intellect she has too, a quick, sprightly one. . . . She is a genuine woman. . . . It is no use doubting or rolling it over in my thoughts. By George! I am in love with her!"

Lucy and Rutherford around the time of their marriage

Hayes proposed marriage to Lucy in June 1851. "On a sudden the impluse seized me," he later exclaimed. "I grasped her hand hastily in my own and with a smile, but earnestly and in quick accents said, 'I love you.' " Gladly, Lucy accepted. Finally, after a long engagement, thirty-year-old Rutherford B. Hayes and twenty-one-year-old Lucy Webb were wed in Cincinnati on December 30, 1852.

The loving couple settled in Cincinnati. "A better wife I never hoped to have," Hayes soon declared. "This is indeed life." The birth of his first son, Birchard, in 1853 pleased Hayes deeply. "I am moving along quietly and happily," he wrote to a cousin in 1855. "My wife and boy

Hayes's beloved sister, Fanny

are my treasures." Together Rutherford and Lucy would
have eight children, although three of them would die of
childhood illnesses.

No death shook Hayes more deeply, however, than that
of his beloved sister in 1856. Fanny Hayes Platt died after
giving birth to twins, who also failed to survive. "Oh what
a blow it is!" grieved Hayes in a letter after he learned the
tragic news. "During all my life she has been the dear
one. . . . My heart bleeds and tears flow as I write." In his
diary he penned, "May her precious memory serve to
make me better, purer, truer, in every relation of life—a
better husband, father, friend and citizen."

Chapter 3

Hayes of the
Twenty-Third Ohio

While Hayes adjusted to the loss of his sister, his law career continued to prosper. His able defense work in three murder trials marked him as a man of fairness. Recognizing his Harvard training, other Cincinnati lawyers sometimes sought Hayes's legal advice on cases.

Lucy Hayes vigorously opposed southern slavery, and her husband naturally agreed. Just across the river from the slave state of Kentucky, Cincinnati was a refuge for many escaped slaves. An antislavery organization called the Underground Railroad helped fugitive slaves win their freedom by any methods it could. When legal aid was needed in Cincinnati, the Underground Railroad often called upon Rutherford Hayes. At all hours, day and night, Hayes hurried to court to offer his assistance. "There was a period," he later remembered, "when I never went to bed without expecting to be called out. . . ."

One of the many factories in the industrial North

In 1858, the sudden death of the city solicitor (attorney) of Cincinnati left that office vacant. To fill the job the city council finally chose Rutherford B. Hayes. The decision received general praise. One Cincinnati newspaper commented, "It would have been very difficult to have made any other selection. . . ." Hayes performed his duties as city attorney so well that in 1859 he was elected to a full two-year term.

Throughout the United States, arguments about slavery were now raging more than ever. With European immigrants working in the many factories of the industrial North, northerners had no use for slaves. Many

Slaves working a cotton plantation in the South

people insisted that slavery be outlawed. Southerners, however, depended upon slavery for the success of their farming economy. It was the slaves who toiled in plantation fields, picking their masters' cotton crops.

The problem reached its final crisis in November 1860 with the election of Abraham Lincoln of Illinois as sixteenth U.S. president. Angry southerners feared that Lincoln planned to abolish slavery. Rather than submit, eleven southern states quit the Union. Together they formed the Confederate States of America and picked Jefferson Davis to be their president.

President Abraham Lincoln

Through the early months of 1861, war fever gripped the country. Then in April Confederate troops bombarded Fort Sumter in the harbor of Charleston, South Carolina, forcing the surrender of the Union garrison. Vowing to hold the nation together, President Lincoln promptly called upon loyal volunteers to put down the rebellion. Thirty-eight-year-old Hayes excitedly marched in the dusty streets of Cincinnati with an informal drill company. Soon he decided he must join the Northern army and help in the war to save the Union. "I would prefer to go into it," he declared, "if I knew I was to die . . . than to live through and after it without taking any part in it."

The Twenty-Third Ohio Volunteer Infantry color guard

Hayes hastened to the Ohio capital of Columbus and assisted in organizing the Twenty-Third Ohio Volunteer Infantry Regiment. Governor William Dennison rewarded Hayes by appointing him major of the regiment. At Camp Chase outside Columbus, the raw recruits learned how to be soldiers. The troops almost rioted when they learned they must use rusty old muskets. Major Hayes made a hurried speech pleading with the men to accept the muskets until better weapons arrived. His patriotic words swayed the crowd, and the crisis passed when one soldier finally yelled, "Bully for Hayes . . . let's get our guns."

Beyond the Ohio River, the western part of Virginia (soon to become the new state of West Virginia) was a "border" region between North and South. Both Union and Confederate armies hoped to control it. In the summer of 1861 the Twenty-Third Ohio and other Union regiments marched into West Virginia's Kanawha River Valley. From the very start Hayes loved army life. Hiking mountain trails and cutting encampments among the forest trees seemed great fun to him. Watching the regiment on parade filled his heart with joy. Even the thought of battle failed to dampen his high spirits. "I shall come safely out of this war," he had promised Lucy when he first left home.

The men of the Twenty-Third Ohio first heard the roar of cannon fire at the Battle of Carnifex Ferry on September 10, 1861. As bullets whistled overhead, Hayes compared his nervousness to what "I have felt before beginning an important lawsuit." In October his gallant service to the regiment earned him a promotion to lieutenant colonel. During the following months the fight for West Virginia seesawed back and forth in a dozen mountain skirmishes. Repeatedly Hayes's bravery under fire impressed his troops. At Giles Court House in May 1862, screaming Confederate soldiers charged ahead as they made a surprise attack upon the Twenty-Third Ohio. Bullets and cannon shells whined through the air, and one shell fragment slightly cut Hayes across his right knee. "Boys, it is getting rather hot here," he calmly stated; "we had better move down." Under his skillful direction, the men retreated to a stronger position.

The wounded Hayes lying on the battlefield

August 26, 1862, found the Twenty-Third Ohio rattling by train into Washington, D.C., to help combat the Confederate army. Now in full command of the Twenty-Third Ohio, Hayes marched his men toward South Mountain, Maryland. If the Yankees could smash through the mountain passes there, they could get behind Lee's army and perhaps destroy it. On September 14, 1862, the infantrymen of the Twenty-Third Ohio yelled and charged toward Fox's Gap. Ferociously Hayes waved his sword and led the way into the thick of the fight.

"Give them Hell!" he loudly commanded, when a musket ball suddenly tore into his left arm. In shock Hayes fell to the ground. Still he shouted orders to his troops. Bullets splattered the earth around him, but by a miracle he received no further injury. At last soldiers carried their wounded commander from the field, but his valiant efforts had helped capture Fox's Gap.

Major Joseph T. Webb,
Hayes's brother-in-law

For weeks after the battle at South Mountain, Hayes lay
in bed in a Middletown, Maryland house. The careful
medical treatment of Hayes's brother-in-law, Doctor
Joseph Webb, and the loving attention of Lucy Hayes when
she finally reached him, saved Hayes's arm and probably
his life. On his fortieth birthday, his arm in a sling, Hayes
walked over the quiet battlefield again with his wife.

Hayes's leadership won him another promotion, this
time to full colonel. "Colonel," Hayes would declare in
later years. "It is the best sounding title I know." In
November the proud soldier rejoined his regiment in West
Virginia. Encamped for the winter, Hayes invited Lucy to
stay with him. Some evenings the regimental band

Winter quarters of the Twenty-Third Ohio at Camp Reynolds, West Virginia

serenaded the colonel and his wife. The Hayeses treated the soldiers of the Twenty-Third Ohio with consideration and affection. They grew especially fond of a young lieutenant named William McKinley, who would also one day become president of the United States.

Skirmishes in West Virignia kept Hayes and his Ohio troops occupied during 1863. Named a brigade commander in 1864, Hayes returned to Virginia leading 2,000 Ohioans and West Virginians. "All things point to early action," he predicted as they joined the Union army forming in the Shenandoah Valley. In fighting at Cloyd's Mountain, Hayes galloped before his men shouting such lively encouragement that one soldier remarked that the colonel seemed "heated clear through." Through the summer, Hayes's personal valor inspired his troops repeatedly.

Left: A formal portrait
of Hayes in uniform

Below: The Battle of
Cedar Creek, Virginia,
on October 19, 1864

Ohioans proudly read newspaper stories of Hayes's heroic army career. With the 1864 elections approaching, politicians in Cincinnati decided Hayes would be the perfect candidate to run for Congress in their district. Happily Hayes accepted the nomination. He steadfastly refused, however, to return to Ohio to campaign. "Thanks. I have other business just now," he explained. "Any man who would leave the army at this time to electioneer for Congress ought to be scalped."

Instead, Hayes remained in the Union Army of the Shenandoah commanded by General Philip Sheridan. At the battles of Opequon and Fisher's Hill he stirred his men to victory. At the same time, in the streets of Cincinnati and in surrounding towns, Republican campaigners paraded for the absent Hayes.

The news of his easy win in the October election reached Hayes in the field. On October 19, 1864, desperate fighting occurred at Cedar Creek, Virginia. "My horse was killed instantly," Hayes later exclaimed. The horse crashed, violently throwing the colonel to the ground unconscious. From a distance, witnesses saw him lying motionless and guessed that he was dead. Newspapers even printed his death notice. Before Lucy could hear this terrible rumor, one of Hayes's captains hurried off a telegram. "The report that your husband was killed this morning is untrue." Altogether during the war Hayes suffered five bullet wounds and had four horses shot from under him. As a result of his "gallant . . . services" at Opequon, Fisher's Hill, and Cedar Creek, Hayes proudly sewed the stars of a brigadier general upon his shoulders.

Chapter 4

The Ohio Politician

"I shall never come to Washington until I can come by way of Richmond," Hayes vowed. Before taking office, he was determined to see the Confederate capital fall. Though elected to Congress, the general remained in the army until the very end of the war. After four long years, the Confederate States of America tottered on the verge of collapse. Southern factories lay destroyed in heaps of rubble. Scorched farms sent clouds of sparks and smoke drifting into the southern skies. Hungry and exhausted, General Robert E. Lee's gray-clad army at last abandoned the Confederate capital in Richmond, Virginia, in April 1865. Within a week Lee was forced to surrender to Union general Ulysses S. Grant in the village of Appomattox Court House.

General Hayes celebrated the wonderful news in West Virginia. He was stunned and saddened when on April 15 he received word that an assassin, John Wilkes Booth, had murdered President Lincoln. The Civil War was over. The nation had been reunited and all the slaves were free. But hard feelings in the North and South would take many years to heal.

Opposite page: Hayes in 1866
as a member of Congress

Hayes at the dedication of a monument to his fallen volunteers

His military duties done, Hayes resigned from the army
on June 8, 1865. When Congress went into session in
December, Hayes walked through the Capitol rotunda and
at last took his seat in the House of Representatives. As a
new congressman Hayes was assigned to work on the
unimportant Library Committee. Elected committee chairman, he designed a bill to expand the Library of Congress
and open its shelves to more readers. When seated in the
House chamber, Hayes often remained quiet and obser-
vant. "He was not a leading debater or manager in party
tactics," one fellow congressman remembered, "but was
always sensible, industrious, and true to his convictions."

Congressman Hayes speaking with freed slaves

In the wake of the Civil War, President Andrew Johnson had hoped to reunite the North and South smoothly. Many bitter northern Republicans, however, wished to punish the South. Gaining control of Congress, these Radical Republicans openly insulted Johnson and fought his Reconstruction policies for rebuilding the South. As a loyal party member, Hayes usually sided with the Republican leadership. He promoted laws that helped freed southern blacks, even though the laws sometimes denied southern whites their constitutional rights. In 1866 satisfied voters in his Ohio district elected him to a second two-year term.

Hayes in 1868, when he was governor of Ohio

The upheaval of Reconstruction dismayed Hayes. Without his family he also felt lonely in Washington. In time he wrote his wife, "Politics is a bad trade. . . . Guess we'll quit." In the summer of 1867 he found a way to escape national politics when Ohio Republicans chose him to run for governor. Hayes resigned from Congress and crisscrossed Ohio during the hard autumn campaign. His impressive war record, warm personality, and honest politics carried him to victory by a majority of 3,000 votes.

"I am enjoying the new office," he soon wrote his Uncle Sardis. "It strikes me as the pleasantest I have ever had. Not too much hard work, plenty of time to read, good society, etc." Governor Hayes possessed little power to pass

University Hall at Ohio State University, around 1874

new laws. During his years as governor the Democrats controlled the Ohio legislature. He did make a number of government appointments, though, and he always insisted on choosing qualified people regardless of their political parties. As one friend later declared, "Hayes attracted good men, freezing the bad."

Honestly he trimmed the state's debt by 20 percent and urged state voter registration to prevent cheating on election days. Train passengers praised Hayes for supporting safe and fair railroad regulations in Ohio. Coal diggers thanked him for promoting better mining safety codes in the state. While governor he also improved conditions in Ohio's prisons and mental hospitals. His interest in education led him to help establish Ohio State University.

43

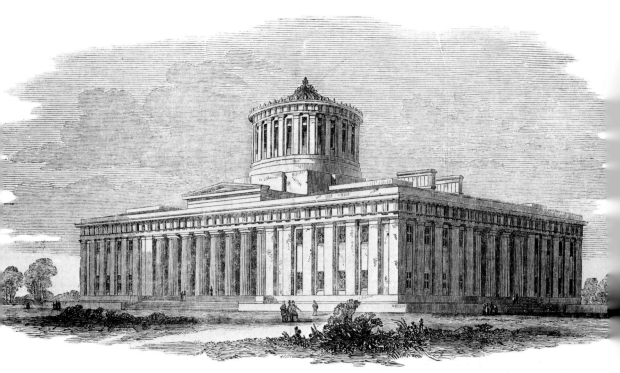

The Ohio state capitol building

In Ohio it was a tradition that governors serve no more than two terms in a row. Accordingly, Hayes left office in January 1872. "I long for freedom and independence," he admitted. "My family and private affairs will be my care hereafter. . . . No more ambition."

Ohio Republicans, however, demanded that forty-nine-year-old Hayes run for a congressional seat again. Against his better judgment, he agreed. Four years of national government under Republican president Ulysses S. Grant had proven a disaster. All across the United States, citizens now grumbled about government corruption, which they correctly blamed on the Republicans. Republican Reconstruction laws left the South in political shambles. With military protection, northern Republicans called carpetbaggers swarmed the southern states. Often crooked, they openly bought the support of black voters while robbing state treasuries.

The gracious Hayes residence in Fremont, Ohio

President Grant remained personally popular and he won reelection in November. Disgusted voters defeated many other Republicans that year, however. In southern Ohio, even Rutherford B. Hayes's unquestioned honesty failed to help him. On election day he was beaten by his Democratic opponent. President Grant offered Hayes a position as an assistant U.S. treasurer, but the Ohioan turned him down. Instead he retired to the quiet life of Fremont, Ohio.

In Fremont, Sardis Birchard had given his famous nephew a handsome estate called Spiegel Grove. In its rambling red brick house, Hayes enjoyed many happy hours reading. On its broad green lawns he liked to stroll and watch his youngest two children play. As he observed continued corruption among the Republicans nationwide, he sourly commented, "I do not sympathize with a large share of the party leaders."

As the 1875 race for Ohio governor neared, state Republicans clearly understood the need for an honest candidate. "I think we must take Hayes," declared Ohio congressman James Garfield at one political meeting. "I am kept for an hour or two daily replying to letters importuning me to run for governor," Hayes soon reported. In his diary he confessed, "A third term would be a distinction — a feather I would like to wear."

At their state convention in 1875, Republicans cheered the nomination of Hayes for Ohio governor. To win a third term as governor, Hayes stumped hard across the state. Paper money backed by gold was one important campaign issue. Voters also argued about public education. In one speech Hayes exclaimed, "Our motto is honest money for all and free schools for all." Newspapers closely covered the Ohio race and Hayes received national attention. Many Republican leaders hinted that, if he won the Ohio election, an even brighter future lay before him. "If victorious," Hayes remarked in his diary, "I am likely to be pushed for the Republican nomination for President." Family members at Spiegel Grove smiled with hope when Hayes won the governor's chair by 5,500 votes.

Above: The Hayes residence at Spiegel Grove (see Hayeses in center window)
Below: The bedroom of Rutherford and Lucy Hayes at Spiegel Grove

Chapter 5

The Disputed Election

"For President in 1876, Rutherford B. Hayes," declared the *Atlantic Monthly* magazine in its March 24 issue. As Republicans searched for a presidential candidate, growing numbers praised the Ohio governor as the best possible choice. Hayes's reputation for complete honesty attracted many voters. Ohio senator John Sherman exclaimed, ". . . considering all things, I believe the nomination of Governor Hayes would give us more strength, taking the whole country at large, than any other man." The *New York Sun* trumpeted, "He is a man of talent; he is a gentleman; he is rich and independent; he served with credit as a soldier in the war, and his record as Governor of Ohio is without flaw or spot. . . ." By May 1876 Supreme Court Chief Justice Morrison Waite believed, "Hayes chances are now decidedly the best of any in the field."

Not everyone supported Hayes, of course. Congressman James G. Blaine of Maine headed a list of half a dozen popular candidates. On June 14, 1876, excited Republican delegates crowded into Exposition Hall in Cincinnati for the start of their national convention.

Opposite page: An 1877 photograph of Hayes 49

Young Webb Hayes attended and soon reported to his father, "Greatest good feeling prevails toward you on all sides. . . . The Ohio men are jubilant. . . ." In the great hall, Ohioans wearing Hayes buttons and badges waved Hayes banners to boost their "favorite son" candidate. Other delegates discussed Blaine's embarrassing involvement in a recent railroad bribery scandal. On the second day of the convention, Webb Hayes wrote to his father again: "If Blaine is not nominated by the 4th ballot your nomination is considered to be certain."

Tensions rose as the day for voting arrived. On the first ballot, Blaine edged within 27 votes of winning the nomination. Of the other candidates, Hayes ranked only fifth in number of votes. Other ballots failed to win Blaine a majority. By the fifth tally, enough votes had shifted to thrust Hayes into second place. The seventh ballot turned the tide. Supporting Hayes as the best compromise candidate, delegates awarded him a majority of 384 votes to Blaine's 351. For twenty minutes wild cheers welcomed the nomination of Rutherford B. Hayes for president. For vice-president the delegates picked New York congressman William Wheeler.

Several days later, Democratic delegates gathered at their convention in Saint Louis, Missouri. They selected New York governor Samuel Tilden to be their presidential candidate. While he was a New York district attorney, Tilden had broken the corrupt political ring of New York City's Tammany Hall. A jury sentenced its leader, "Boss" William Tweed, to jail. Men who fought public dishonesty at this time were called "reformers." As a reform gover-

Republican banner for the 1876 presidential campaign

nor, Tilden continued the battle against corruption in his state. His reputation for honesty easily equaled that of Hayes.

Tilden vowed to replace the crookedness in Washington with honest government. "Throw the Rascals Out!" yelled Democratic supporters as they paraded through the streets. Tilden also insisted that the harsh Reconstruction policies forced by Congress upon the South be ended. The ex-Confederate states had been punished enough for their actions during the Civil War.

Governor Hayes stated his own political views in a bold "Letter of Acceptance" to his nomination. Republicans in President Grant's administration had believed, "To the victors belong the spoils." They awarded government jobs only to loyal party members regardless of their skills. Hayes condemned this "spoils system" and promised to fill offices with qualified Republicans and Democrats alike. To prevent corrupting influences, he stated he would serve only one four-year term if elected. He pledged to put forward "a civil policy which will wipe out forever the distinction between North and South in our common country." Reform Republican Carl Schurz read the Letter of Acceptance and warned Hayes that it was bound to "displease some very powerful men in your own party." "Yes, that may be so," calmly answered Hayes, "but it is right."

"Hurrah! For Hayes and Honest Ways!" chanted Republican supporters. "Tilden and Reform!" answered yelling Democrats. During the hard-fought summer campaign, voters gathered in town squares and listened to fiery Republican speakers. These politicians accused Tilden of cheating on his income tax and secretly favoring slavery. They wondered aloud what Tilden was doing in New York while Hayes fought patriotically on southern battlefields for the Union. Calling Tilden a thief and a liar, Republicans nicknamed him "Slippery Sammy."

The Democrats attacked Hayes with equal fury. They claimed he stole the watches of dead soldiers during the war. They said that Hayes, while governor, had wasted money in the Ohio treasury. Some Democrats even raved that Hayes had shot his mother "in a fit of insanity."

Above: The Tilden-Hendricks campaign banner
Below: A Democratic campaign procession in New York City

Both Hayes and Tilden disapproved of such lying campaign tactics. There was little they could do to stop them, however. Following tradition, the two candidates rarely appeared in public. The year 1876 marked the one-hundredth year of American independence. Through the summer and fall, proud citizens flocked to the grand Centennial Exposition in Philadelphia, Pennsylvania. In October even Governor Hayes traveled east to see exhibits celebrating America's national progress. Visitors crowded close to glimpse the presidential candidate, but many were disappointed by his plain appearance. His beard looked uncombed, and a *New York Times* reporter noticed that he wore "a dreadfully shabby coat and a shockingly bad hat. . . ." Honest Rutherford B. Hayes made no effort to be anything more than a simple man of the people.

As the tough 1876 election campaign neared its end, few Americans could guess who would win. "The contest is close and yet doubtful," remarked Hayes in his diary, "with the chances, as I see them, rather against us." At last election day arrived on November 7. In the parlor of the house he rented in Columbus, Governor Hayes waited with family and friends. Through the evening, telegraph messengers hurriedly delivered the latest election results.

From the very start the news was bad. Hayes carried Ohio only by a very close margin. Many other states cast their votes for Tilden. "The effect was depressing," admitted Hayes as he received other unofficial bulletins. In the popular vote Tilden seemed the clear winner. The final tally would give Tilden 4,284,757 votes to Hayes's 4,033,950. As Hayes counted the all-important electoral votes from each state, he guessed Tilden would win the needed majority of 185.

Shortly after midnight, Hayes wearily climbed the stairs to his bedroom. He prepared for sleep, convinced of his defeat "after a very close contest." Many others believed Hayes had lost as well. In New York City, excited Democrats thronged outside Tilden's mansion carrying torches and waving flags. Telegrams poured in with Democratic messages of congratulations such as "Bully for us!" and "Reform at last!" In Indiana, during the hours of early morning, the presses at the Republican *Indianapolis Journal* printed the next day's news: "With the result before us at this writing we see no escape from the conclusion that Tilden . . . [is] elected. . . ."

Some Republicans, however, refused to accept defeat. In New York City John Reid, managing editor of *The New York Times*, and Michigan senator Zachariah Chandler, the Republican national chairman, carefully examined state election returns. Soon Chandler dashed off a telegram to the Republican governor of South Carolina: "HAYES IS ELECTED IF WE HAVE CARRIED SOUTH CAROLINA, FLORIDA AND LOUISIANA. CAN YOU HOLD YOUR STATE? ANSWER IMMEDIATELY." Trusted Republican officials in Florida and Louisiana received similar messages. If Hayes could capture all the electoral votes of these critical states, plus one disputed vote from Oregon, he would have exactly the number needed to win the election. Hurrying back to his office, editor Reid prepared bold words for the November 9 edition of *The New York Times*: "Hayes has 185 electoral votes and is elected."

Republicans and Democrats quickly took sides on the important issue. As a result of Reconstruction, South Carolina, Florida, and Louisiana remained under federal military control. Union soldiers guarded the halls of these three southern statehouses and kept Republican carpetbag politicians in power. Democrats insisted that corrupt Republicans had stuffed the ballot boxes with false votes so that Hayes would carry those three states. Republicans, in turn, claimed that the secret white terrorist group called the Ku Klux Klan had been at work the night before the election. Disguised in ghostly robes and high peaked hoods, Klansmen had beaten blacks and burned their houses. By frightening black Republican voters from voting, they hoped to insure victory for Tilden.

As tensions flared, both Republicans and Democrats rushed representatives south to supervise the count of election returns and guard against fraud. President Grant ordered more troops into the three crucial states "to preserve peace and good order." In spite of these precautions, cheating undoubtedly occurred on both sides. Rumors of bribed voting officials, forged ballots, and beaten black voters filtered up to the North.

Amid the confusion, Hayes revealed his own feelings to Senator Sherman: "A fair election would have given us about forty electoral votes at the South—at least that many. But we are not to allow our friends to defeat one outrage and fraud by another. There must be nothing crooked on our part." When hopeful reports arrived from Louisiana, Hayes declared, "I have no doubt that we are justly and legally entitled to the Presidency."

56

Right: Members of the
Ku Klux Klan in their
robes in Alabama, 1868

Below: Plantation hands
on their way to the polls
in South Carolina, 1876

Fraudulent voters in custody at the U.S. Circuit Court, New York, 1876

In the end both the Republicans and Democrats of South Carolina, Florida, and Louisiana submitted separate sets of voting results. The U.S. Constitution states that "The President of the Senate shall in the Presence of the Senate and House of Representatives, open all the Certificates, and the [electoral] Votes shall then be counted." It did not explain, however, who would count the votes. If given the chance, the Republican president of the Senate would, of course, have accepted the returns supporting Hayes. The Democrats, who comprised the majority of the members in Congress, refused to agree to that. As the winter days passed, Republican and Democratic politicians feverishly searched for a compromise solution.

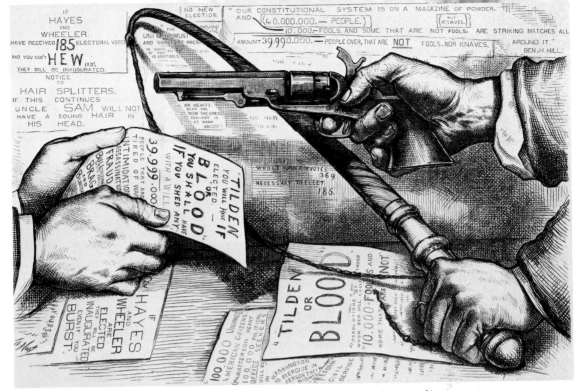

An 1877 political cartoon on the violence of the election dispute

Across the nation, furious Democrats claimed the election was being stolen from them. Where Democratic mobs gathered, they yelled "Tilden or Blood" and "Tilden or War." Democratic state militiamen counted their guns and bullets and readied their companies to spring into action. Kentucky congressman Henry Watterson loudly threatened to march 100,000 Democrats to Washington to see that Tilden received justice.

In Columbus, Governor Hayes's daily mail contained ugly personal threats. One anonymous letter warned him to remember what had happened to Lincoln. One evening during dinner, a bullet burst through the Hayes parlor window. It passed through two rooms before burrowing into the library wall. No one knew if it was an accident or a murder attempt. After that, Webb Hayes carried a pistol when he accompanied his father on his evening strolls.

Through these days of political turmoil, Samuel Tilden remained peaceable. In response to Democratic talk of violence, the New York governor replied, "It will not do to fight. We have just emerged from one civil war, and it will never do to engage in another civil war; it would end in the destruction of free government."

At last Congress found a way to solve the election dispute by establishing a special Electoral Commission. Composed of five senators, five representatives, and five justices of the Supreme Court, the commission contained seven Republicans and seven Democrats. The fifteenth member, Republican Supreme Court Justice Joseph Bradley, was thought to be politically independent. People hoped his presence would insure a fair result.

On February 1, 1877, excited observers packed the Capitol as the electoral count began in the House of Representatives. Of the disputed votes, Tilden needed only one to win the presidential contest. Through the next tense days, every time a decision needed to be made, however, Justice Bradley sided with his fellow Republicans. As a result, by decisions of eight to seven, all the electoral votes of South Carolina, Florida, and Louisiana, and one from Oregon, were awarded to Hayes.

Democrats fumed as they saw events turning against them. The *Cincinnati Enquirer* called the work of the Electoral Commission "the monster fraud of the century." The U.S. Constitution required every four-year presidential term to begin on March 4. Now frustrated Democratic congressmen threatened to stall the count until after March 4, throwing the leaderless nation into chaos.

The Electoral Commission meeting to resolve the disputed election

To prevent such an obstacle, the Republicans quickly bargained to make southern Democrats happier. At secret meetings and in huddled whispers, Republican leaders pledged in Hayes's behalf to withdraw the last of the federal troops from the South, spend more national money in the southern states, and invite at least one southerner into the next cabinet. At the same time, to avoid further conflict, Tilden nobly insisted Democrats accept the verdicts of the Electoral Commission.

Thomas Ferry declares Rutherford B. Hayes the victor.

At 4:10 in the morning of March 2, 1877, just two days before inauguration day, the final count of the electoral vote occurred in the House of Representatives. It awarded Rutherford B. Hayes 185 votes and Samuel Tilden 184 votes. His voice echoing through the House chamber, Michigan senator Thomas W. Ferry (the president of the Senate) announced: "Rutherford B. Hayes, having received the majority of the whole number of electoral votes, is duly elected President of the United States." Witnesses rushed along the Capitol corridors to spread the historic news.

HERE
LIES
THE
DEMOCRATIC
TIGER.
GREATLY MOURNED
BY THE BEREAVED
FILIBUSTERS.

A battered elephant, symbol of the Republican party, licks its wounds after its election victory.

The day before, on March 1, Hayes departed for Washington without knowing if he had been elected or not. At the Columbus railroad station he smiled at the gathered crowd and joked that "perhaps" he would "be back immediately." Through the next hours Hayes's train rolled eastward. At dawn on March 2 the train chugged to a stop near Harrisburg, Pennsylvania. An excited messenger boarded and awoke Hayes with a telegram: he clearly had been elected. The fight for the presidency had ended. In this moment of triumph, kindly Rutherford B. Hayes thought not of himself but of others. As friends and family wildly cheered the wonderful news, he gently scolded, "Boys, boys . . . you'll wake the passengers."

63

Above: Hayes meets the first Chinese minister to the United States.
Below: Hayes stops for a photo during a train trip to the West.

Above: The Hayes party on a stagecoach ride through Yosemite, California
Below: The Hayes family spending an enjoyable evening in the White House

Above: Rutherford B. Hayes and two of his sons
Opposite page: Rutherford and Lucy Webb Hayes

Chapter 6

His Fraudulency

Monday, March 5, 1877, dawned cool and cloudy in Washington, D.C. Still, thirty thousand eager citizens jammed the Capitol grounds to witness the inauguration of Rutherford B. Hayes as nineteenth U.S. president. In truth, Hayes was already president. Because inauguration day landed on a Sunday that year, Hayes secretly took the oath of office on Saturday evening, March 3. During a private White House dinner he quietly stepped into the Red Room. Raising his right hand before Supreme Court Chief Justice Waite, Hayes swore to "preserve and protect" the U.S. Constitution.

On March 5, however, the fifty-four-year-old Ohioan took the oath again in the traditional public ceremony. Just after noon, Hayes walked out onto the Capitol's east portico. "His step was firm and his eyes were bright," reported the *Chicago Tribune.* Carefully people listened as he gave his inaugural address. In a strong, clear voice Hayes pledged fair treatment for all Americans, whites and blacks, northerners and southerners. He also promised to give Americans honest, skilled government even if it sometimes hurt his Republican party. "He serves his party best who serves his country best," he exclaimed.

Democratic congressmen refused to attend the inauguration ceremony. Most Democrats still insisted that Hayes had no right to be president. They bitterly called him "His Fraudulency," "The Fraudulent President," and "Ruther-*fraud* B. Hayes." Under these difficult circumstances Hayes settled into the White House. As he took over the leadership of the government he vowed, "I shall show a *grit* that will astonish those who predict weakness."

Hayes's character was strictly honorable. Hoping to unite the North and South, he agreed to fulfill the political bargains that had made him president. In his cabinet he named a southern Democrat, David M. Key of Tennessee, as postmaster general. In South Carolina, U.S. infantrymen still patrolled the statehouse corridors. On April 3, 1877, Hayes instructed the Secretary of War: "You are . . . directed to see that the proper orders are issued for the removal of said troops from the State House." When similar orders soon marched the last soldiers from the statehouse in Louisiana, Reconstruction came to an end. Defeated Republican politicians packed their carpetbags and returned north.

Southern white Democrats quickly took control of their state governments. President Hayes had said, "My policy is trust, peace, and to put aside the bayonet." Although he hoped for the best, the rise of white Democratic power in the South had sad results for southern blacks. Angry over Reconstruction and the loss of their slaves, southern whites denied blacks any voice in their state governments. Through the next decades, blacks would be allowed only the rights of second-class citizens.

A cartoon on Hayes's announcement of an era of peace and trust

In a further attempt to heal the wounds of the Civil War, Hayes urged that federal money be spent to help rebuild the South. Soon work crews chopped trees and cleared the way for new roads across the southern states. Southern construction gangs hammered together bridges, dredged waterways, and dug canals to transport produce more easily. Such internal improvements brightened the future for many southerners. Some northern newspapers complained about the "looting of the treasury for the former rebels." But while Republicans grumbled, Democrats called Hayes "the greatest Southerner of the day."

Since 1873 the United States had been gripped by a financial panic. To protect their companies, several railroad owners in 1877 cut their workers' pay. Rather than accept wages of less than $1.50 a day, one union, the Brotherhood of Locomotive Engineers, angrily urged its members to strike. Soon railroad machinists and trackmen threw down their tools and joined the engineers on picket lines. When the railroad owners hired nonunion men to keep the trains running, America's first full-scale labor crisis erupted in July 1877.

Across the nation strikers rioted. They torched freight cars and ripped up tracks. In pitched battles, strikers hurled rocks and sticks, and the police responded with gunfire. The continued fighting caused millions of dollars' worth of damage and left scores of people dead. When state militiamen failed to stop the violence, the governors of West Virginia, Maryland, Pennsylvania, and Illinois appealed to President Hayes for help. "The whole country will soon be in . . . revolution unless you can save it by prompt action," pleaded Governor Hartranft of Pennsylvania. At last Hayes sent federal troops to halt the strike and restore peace. His forceful action ended the Great Railroad Strike of 1877.

To root out crookedness in the federal government, Hayes tried his best to make appointments based on merit instead of unfair influence. The old spoils system "ought to be abolished," he declared. "The reform should be thorough, radical, and complete." "Let appointments and removals," he added, "be made on business principles and fixed rules."

Above: Rioters burn a railroad bridge during the Great Railroad Strike.
Below: The Sixth Maryland Regiment with railroad strikers in Baltimore

Unwilling to give up the jobs they controlled, Republican leaders resisted all of the president's reform efforts. They raged when Hayes issued an executive order in June 1877. The order forbade federal workers from holding posts in political organizations at the same time. The New York City customs collector, Chester A. Arthur, openly refused to quit his Republican activities. After a long fight with Congress, Hayes finally removed Arthur from the customs office.

Through Hayes's first years in Washington, many Democrats still claimed he had cheated to win the presidency. One day, however, a newspaperwoman visited the White House and met the Hayes family. "They don't look like . . . people who would lend themselves to fraud of any kind," she honestly reported. Indeed, Rutherford, Lucy, and their children showed themselves to be a simple, close-knit, loving family. They also brought fresh enthusiasm to the White House.

Each morning President Hayes rose at 7:00 A.M. and stretched and exercised before briskly walking in the White House garden. After a light breakfast and prayers, he turned to work. Through the morning, congressmen and government officials trooped into his office for meetings. In the afternoons Hayes wrote letters and often enjoyed a relaxing carriage ride through the streets of Washington.

Webb Hayes served as his father's personal secretary. The two other older boys, Birchard and Rutherford, were often away at college. The youngest Hayes children, Fanny and Scott, however, filled the White House with fun as

Scott and Fanny Hayes with their nanny, Winnie Monroe

they played in the halls or scampered on the lawn among the chickens that pecked there. On many evenings, family and friends gathered around a piano to sing hymns and other popular melodies. It was on holidays that the glad spirits of the Hayes family most affected observers. White House paymaster William Crook remembered, "It was a real Christmas that came to the White House in those days and Mrs. Hayes's smile was better than eggnog."

The Easter Egg Roll on the White House lawn

The activities of Lucy Hayes certainly excited the country. The president's attractive, cheerful wife filled the White House with old-fashioned American virtues. When Washington children were turned away from their traditional Easter-egg-rolling contests on the Capitol grounds, Lucy Hayes promptly invited them to use the White House lawn instead. Thanks to her, the annual Easter Egg Roll has been a White House custom ever since. Reporter Mary Clemmer Ames referred to Lucy Hayes as the "first lady of the land." In the following years the new title "First Lady" would be applied to all of the presidential wives.

No other First Lady ever had graduated from college. With educated views on religion, women's rights, and national affairs, Lucy Hayes often influenced her husband.

A romantic portrait of Lucy Hayes

Together the Hayeses threw Washington into an uproar when they decided to outlaw alcohol at the White House. Americans who enjoyed drinking liquor teasingly nicknamed Mrs. Hayes "Lemonade Lucy." Official White House dinners without alcohol became the source of many Washington jokes. "It was a brilliant event," remarked Secretary of State William M. Evarts after one affair; "the water flowed like champagne." A sympathetic steward sometimes secretly served a frozen rum punch to thirsty dinner guests. Drinkers came to call this dinner course the "Life-Saving Station." To signal the end of many quiet cold-water dinners, the Marine Corps Band played "Home Sweet Home" at ten o'clock sharp.

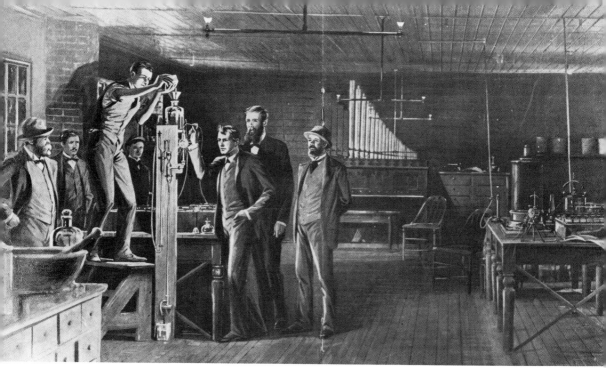

The first incandescent light bulb glows in Edison's Menlo Park laboratory.

One night, though, in April 1878, Hayes stayed up well beyond that hour. Thirty-one-year-old Thomas A. Edison arrived at the White House to demonstrate his new invention, the phonograph. President Hayes and other wide-eyed guests listened as the phonograph played back recorded words and songs. The young inventor did not leave the White House until 3:30 A.M.

In the following year Edison amazed Americans again when he perfected the electric light at his laboratory in Menlo Park, New Jersey. Other advances in American technology also greatly affected the nation during Hayes's presidential years. After testing Alexander Graham Bell's fabulous 1876 invention, Hayes ordered that a telephone be installed at the White House. New techniques in plumbing allowed bathers at the White House to experience running water for the first time. In Chicago in 1877, George Pullman produced a railroad car called the President.

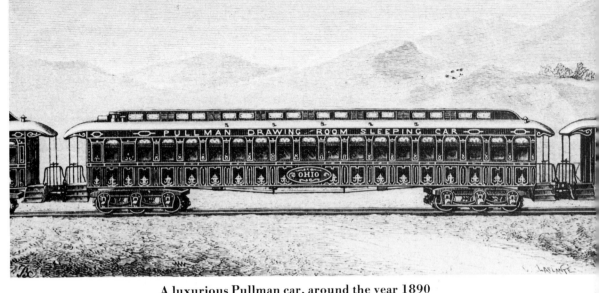

A luxurious Pullman car, around the year 1890

Grateful passengers soon compared the coach, with its comfortable sleeping compartments, to a hotel on wheels. In time thousands of Pullman cars changed the way Americans traveled.

Surely President Hayes climbed aboard Pullman cars during some of his tours across the United States. Hayes traveled so much while in office that the *Chicago Times* dubbed him "Rutherford the Rover." In the western territories, he saw that the nation's peaceful Indians were receiving fairer treatment than ever before on their reservations. In California, laborers thanked the president for protecting their jobs by limiting the number of Chinese immigrants entering the country.

"I am not liked as a President, by the politicians in office, in the press, or in congress," Hayes had once remarked. Common Americans, however, grew to feel differently about the honest Ohioan. After one long trip he observed, "Received everywhere heartily. The country is again one and united! I am very happy to be able to feel that the course taken has turned out so well."

Chapter 7

"Shoving On to the End!"

After struggling for four years with an unfriendly Congress, President Hayes had had enough of Washington. Keeping his campaign promise, he refused to run for a second term. "I am heartily tired of this life of . . . responsibility and toil," he declared. "I wish it was at an end. . . ."

As the campaign season of 1880 approached, a friend remarked to the president, "Well, you will soon be out of it."

"Yes," smiled Hayes, "out of a scrape, out of a scrape."

When the Republican national convention opened in Chicago in June 1880, Hayes followed its progress with interest. After thirty-six ballots, delegates cheered the selection of Hayes's old friend Ohio congressman James A. Garfield. "Garfield's nomination at Chicago," commented Hayes, "was the best that was possible. It is altogether good. . . ." The convention's choice of his old foe Chester A. Arthur for vice-president, however, made Hayes less happy.

The wreath of the presidency passes from Hayes to Garfield.

In the November election Garfield beat his Democratic opponent, General Winfield S. Hancock, by a close margin. The Republicans would remain in power, and Hayes prepared to hand over his office with satisfaction. Thanks to Hayes, the nation was now more united and prosperous than in 1877. Most Americans agreed that he had performed his presidential duties with grace and strength.

On inauguration day, March 4, 1881, Hayes escorted James Garfield to the Capitol. One witness, George Julian, noticed: "Hayes looked as sweet & lamblike as possible . . ." as he watched Garfield take the oath of office.

Earlier Hayes had written, "Nobody ever left the Presidency with less regret, less disappointment, fewer heart burnings, or more general content . . . than I do."

On the evening of March 4, ex-president Hayes departed Washington. A train accident in Baltimore shook up the Hayes family, but at last on March 8 they arrived safely in Fremont. Excited friends and neighbors met Hayes with tooting bands and colorful banners. They paraded beside his carriage as it wheeled out to Spiegel Grove. Glad to be home at last, Hayes looked forward to the pleasures of small-town Ohio. "We wish to get as completely back into private life as we can," he soon explained to a friend.

At Spiegel Grove Hayes looked after personal business affairs, tended his shrubs and fruit trees, and relaxed in the sunshine on his porch. The shooting by an assassin of President Garfield and his death in September 1881 shocked Hayes. "The march of events will go on but it is a personal grief," he exclaimed. As Chester Arthur stepped into the presidency, Hayes followed his progress carefully. Arthur's surprising work as a government reformer gladdened the ex-president.

Even as a private citizen, Hayes felt a duty to assist in public affairs. He served as a director at a local bank and greatly aided the Fremont library with money. Hayes showed his interest in education by becoming a trustee of Ohio State University and other Ohio colleges. As a member of the boards of both the Peabody Education Fund and the Slater Fund, Hayes awarded scholarships to poor black students.

Above: Bystanders grab Garfield's assassin as the wounded president swoons.
Below: A reunion of the Twenty-Third Ohio band in the late 1800s

As the years passed, many people forgot Hayes. One day in New York City, lawyer Chauncey Depew encountered him in front of a grocer's fruit display. Depew greeted him cheerfully and said to the grocer, "That is ex-president Hayes. Don't you want to meet him?" "I am not interested in him," the grocer answered, "but I have the finest collection of pears in the city and want to sell you some."

Members of the Union army veterans' organization, the Grand Army of the Republic, as well as the officers of a group called the Loyal Legion, recognized Hayes much more often. At every opportunity Hayes joined his "old comrades" at reunions. At yearly encampments he pitched his tent with them and proudly marched in their parades.

Clearly Hayes loved being at his Spiegel Grove home the best. With Lucy at his side he lived his retirement years to the fullest. On June 22, 1889, however, fifty-seven-year-old Lucy suffered a sudden stroke that left her barely able to move and completely unable to speak. When Hayes reached her side, he later remembered, "In her old manner, she pressed my hand and tried to smile. . . ." Sadly, though, she soon slipped into a coma, and three days later she died. For weeks following the burial of his dear wife, Hayes wandered mournfully about the gardens at Spiegel Grove. "She is in Heaven," he consoled himself. "She is where all the best of earth have gone."

To ease his grief, Hayes continued to perform his many civic activities with energy. In a September 1890 letter he exclaimed, "I go to West Virginia reunion next week at Parkersburg; to National Prison Congress, Cincinnati, the week after; and the following week Peabody in New York;

13th and 16th of October, Indianapolis and St. Louis, Loyal Legion." In November 1891, the gray old man toured the South. In three weeks he journeyed through six states, visiting schools supported by the Peabody and Slater funds. To a friend he declared, "Busy as ever — busier! Shoving on to the end!"

Hayes's tireless volunteer work finally overcame him in 1893. On January 8, the seventy-year-old ex-president drove a sleigh over the snow-covered ground to visit Lucy's grave. That night he noted in his diary, "My feeling was one of longing to be quietly resting in a grave by her side." The next day he traveled to Columbus for a meeting of the Ohio State University Board of Trustees. While in Columbus he chatted with his old war comrade, governor William McKinley. McKinley's election in 1896 would make him the second veteran of the Twenty-Third Ohio Regiment to become president of the United States.

A chilly train ride carried Hayes onward to Cleveland. In spite of a cough and a bad cold, he conducted more business at Western Reserve University. On January 14 he trudged through deep snow with his son, Webb, to catch the train home to Fremont. While they waited at the station, a severe pain suddenly gripped his chest. He slumped over in shock, and Webb Hayes guessed his father had suffered a heart attack. A glass of brandy relieved the pain somewhat, though Hayes said the hurt reminded him of his war wound at South Mountain. Webb urged his father to rest in Cleveland, but Hayes insisted on boarding the train for Fremont. "I would rather die at Spiegel Grove than to live anywhere else," he said.

A hearse bears Hayes's body from Spiegel Grove to Oakwood Cemetery.

At Spiegel Grove Hayes was helped to bed. His doctor prescribed medicines for the heart ailment and told the patient to rest. Through the next days the old man struggled with his pain. "I know that I am going where Lucy is," he whispered on January 17, 1893—his last recorded words. At eleven o'clock that night his heart gave out, and Rutherford B. Hayes died.

Scores of veterans of the Twenty-Third Ohio stood in the snow and doffed their hats at the funeral of their beloved colonel. Other old soldiers solemnly carried the wooden coffin to its resting place at Fremont's Oakwood Cemetery. There Hayes joined his wife at last, though in 1915 the two would be reburied at Spiegel Grove. Democratic president-elect Grover Cleveland honored the memory of Hayes by attending the wintry funeral. His presence there openly showed that the Democrats no longer considered President Hayes a fraud.

Rutherford Birchard Hayes, 1822-1893

As the nation mourned its loss, other statesmen also paid tribute to the former president. President Benjamin Harrison praised him, saying, "He was a patriot citizen, a lover of our flag and of our free institutions . . . a soldier of dauntless courage, a loyal comrade and friend. . . ." Senator John Sherman summed up the nation's sentiments: "Among the multitude of public men I have met I have known no one who held a higher sense of his duty . . . than President Hayes."

As nineteenth U.S. president, Rutherford B. Hayes never flinched from using his skills and judgment with honesty and fairness. Through war and hard-fought peace, he left his mark upon America.

The Hayes family after a tennis match at Spiegel Grove in 1887

Chronology of American History

(Shaded area covers events in Rutherford B. Hayes's lifetime.)

About A.D. 982—Eric the Red, born in Norway, reaches Greenland in one of the first European voyages to North America.

About 1000—Leif Ericson (Eric the Red's son) leads what is thought to be the first European expedition to mainland North America; Leif probably lands in Canada.

1492—Christopher Columbus, seeking a sea route from Spain to the Far East, discovers the New World.

1497—John Cabot reaches Canada in the first English voyage to North America.

1513—Ponce de León explores Florida in search of the fabled Fountain of Youth.

1519-1521—Hernando Cortés of Spain conquers Mexico.

1534—French explorers led by Jacques Cartier enter the Gulf of St. Lawrence in Canada.

1540—Spanish explorer Francisco Coronado begins exploring the American Southwest, seeking the riches of the mythical Seven Cities of Cibola.

1565—St. Augustine, Florida, the first permanent European town in what is now the United States, is founded by the Spanish.

1607—Jamestown, Virginia, is founded, the first permanent English town in the present-day U.S.

1608—Frenchman Samuel de Champlain founds the village of Quebec, Canada.

1609—Henry Hudson explores the eastern coast of present-day U.S. for the Netherlands; the Dutch then claim parts of New York, New Jersey, Delaware, and Connecticut and name the area New Netherland.

1619—The English colonies' first shipment of black slaves arrives in Jamestown.

1620—English Pilgrims found Massachusetts' first permanent town at Plymouth.

1621—Massachusetts Pilgrims and Indians hold the famous first Thanksgiving feast in colonial America.

1623—Colonization of New Hampshire is begun by the English.

1624—Colonization of present-day New York State is begun by the Dutch at Fort Orange (Albany).

1625—The Dutch start building New Amsterdam (now New York City).

1630—The town of Boston, Massachusetts, is founded by the English Puritans.

1633—Colonization of Connecticut is begun by the English.

1634—Colonization of Maryland is begun by the English.

1636—Harvard, the colonies' first college, is founded in Massachusetts. Rhode Island colonization begins when Englishman Roger Williams founds Providence.

1638—Delaware colonization begins as Swedes build Fort Christina at present-day Wilmington.

1640—Stephen Daye of Cambridge, Massachusetts prints *The Bay Psalm Book*, the first English-language book published in what is now the U.S.

1643—Swedish settlers begin colonizing Pennsylvania.

About 1650—North Carolina is colonized by Virginia settlers.

1660—New Jersey colonization is begun by the Dutch at present-day Jersey City.

1670—South Carolina colonization is begun by the English near Charleston.

1673—Jacques Marquette and Louis Jolliet explore the upper Mississippi River for France.

1682—Philadelphia, Pennsylvania, is settled. La Salle explores Mississippi River all the way to its mouth in Louisiana and claims the whole Mississippi Valley for France.

1693—College of William and Mary is founded in Williamsburg, Virginia.

1700—Colonial population is about 250,000.

1703—Benjamin Franklin is born in Boston.

1732—George Washington, first president of the U.S., is born in Westmoreland County, Virginia.

1733—James Oglethorpe founds Savannah, Georgia; Georgia is established as the thirteenth colony.

1735—John Adams, second president of the U.S., is born in Braintree, Massachusetts.

1737—William Byrd founds Richmond, Virginia.

1738—British troops are sent to Georgia over border dispute with Spain.

1739—Black insurrection takes place in South Carolina.

1740—English Parliament passes act allowing naturalization of immigrants to American colonies after seven-year residence.

1743—Thomas Jefferson is born in Albemarle County, Virginia. Benjamin Franklin retires at age thirty-seven to devote himself to scientific inquiries and public service.

1744—King George's War begins; France joins war effort against England.

1745—During King George's War, France raids settlements in Maine and New York.

1747—Classes begin at Princeton College in New Jersey.

1748—The Treaty of Aix-la-Chapelle concludes King George's War.

1749—Parliament legally recognizes slavery in colonies and the inauguration of the plantation system in the South. George Washington becomes the surveyor for Culpepper County in Virginia.

1750—Thomas Walker passes through and names Cumberland Gap on his way toward Kentucky region. Colonial population is about 1,200,000.

1751—James Madison, fourth president of the U.S., is born in Port Conway, Virginia. English Parliament passes Currency Act, banning New England colonies from issuing paper money. George Washington travels to Barbados.

1752—Pennsylvania Hospital, the first general hospital in the colonies, is founded in Philadelphia. Benjamin Franklin uses a kite in a thunderstorm to demonstrate that lightning is a form of electricity.

1753—George Washington delivers command that the French withdraw from the Ohio River Valley; French disregard the demand. Colonial population is about 1,328,000.

1754—French and Indian War begins (extends to Europe as the Seven Years' War). Washington surrenders at Fort Necessity.

1755—French and Indians ambush Braddock. Washington becomes commander of Virginia troops.

1756—England declares war on France.

1758—James Monroe, fifth president of the U.S., is born in Westmoreland County, Virginia.

1759—Cherokee Indian war begins in southern colonies; hostilities extend to 1761. George Washington marries Martha Dandridge Custis.

1760—George III becomes king of England. Colonial population is about 1,600,000.

1762—England declares war on Spain.

1763—Treaty of Paris concludes the French and Indian War and the Seven Years' War. England gains Canada and most other French lands east of the Mississippi River.

1764—British pass the Sugar Act to gain tax money from the colonists. The issue of taxation without representation is first introduced in Boston. John Adams marries Abigail Smith.

1765—Stamp Act goes into effect in the colonies. Business virtually stops as almost all colonists refuse to use the stamps.

1766—British repeal the Stamp Act.

1767—John Quincy Adams, sixth president of the U.S. and son of second president John Adams, is born in Braintree, Massachusetts. Andrew Jackson, seventh president of the U.S., is born in Waxhaw settlement, South Carolina.

1769—Daniel Boone sights the Kentucky Territory.

1770—In the Boston Massacre, British soldiers kill five colonists and injure six. Townshend Acts are repealed, thus eliminating all duties on imports to the colonies except tea.

1771—Benjamin Franklin begins his autobiography, a work that he will never complete. The North Carolina assembly passes the "Bloody Act," which makes rioters guilty of treason.

1772—Samuel Adams rouses colonists to consider British threats to self-government.

1773—English Parliament passes the Tea Act. Colonists dressed as Mohawk Indians board British tea ships and toss 342 casks of tea into the water in what becomes known as the Boston Tea Party. William Henry Harrison is born in Charles City County, Virginia.

1774—British close the port of Boston to punish the city for the Boston Tea Party. First Continental Congress convenes in Philadelphia.

1775—American Revolution begins with battles of Lexington and Concord, Massachusetts. Second Continental Congress opens in Philadelphia. George Washington becomes commander-in-chief of the Continental army.

1776—Declaration of Independence is adopted on July 4.

1777—Congress adopts the American flag with thirteen stars and thirteen stripes. John Adams is sent to France to negotiate peace treaty.

1778—France declares war against Great Britain and becomes U.S. ally.

1779—British surrender to Americans at Vincennes. Thomas Jefferson is elected governor of Virginia. James Madison is elected to the Continental Congress.

1780—Benedict Arnold, first American traitor, defects to the British.

1781—Articles of Confederation go into effect. Cornwallis surrenders to George Washington at Yorktown, ending the American Revolution.

1782—American commissioners, including John Adams, sign peace treaty with British in Paris. Thomas Jefferson's wife, Martha, dies. Martin Van Buren is born in Kinderhook, New York.

1784—Zachary Taylor is born near Barboursville, Virginia.

1785—Congress adopts the dollar as the unit of currency. John Adams is made minister to Great Britain. Thomas Jefferson is appointed minister to France.

1786—Shays's Rebellion begins in Massachusetts.

1787—Constitutional Convention assembles in Philadelphia, with George Washington presiding; U.S. Constitution is adopted. Delaware, New Jersey, and Pennsylvania become states.

1788—Virginia, South Carolina, New York, Connecticut, New Hampshire, Maryland, and Massachusetts become states. U.S. Constitution is ratified. New York City is declared U.S. capital.

1789—Presidential electors elect George Washington and John Adams as first president and vice-president. Thomas Jefferson is appointed secretary of state. North Carolina becomes a state. French Revolution begins.

1790—Supreme Court meets for the first time. Rhode Island becomes a state. First national census in the U.S. counts 3,929,214 persons. John Tyler is born in Charles City County, Virginia.

1791—Vermont enters the Union. U.S. Bill of Rights, the first ten amendments to the Constitution, goes into effect. District of Columbia is established. James Buchanan is born in Stony Batter, Pennsylvania.

1792—Thomas Paine publishes *The Rights of Man*. Kentucky becomes a state. Two political parties are formed in the U.S., Federalist and Republican. Washington is elected to a second term, with Adams as vice-president.

1793—War between France and Britain begins; U.S. declares neutrality. Eli Whitney invents the cotton gin; cotton production and slave labor increase in the South.

1794—Eleventh Amendment to the Constitution is passed, limiting federal courts' power. "Whiskey Rebellion" in Pennsylvania protests federal whiskey tax. James Madison marries Dolley Payne Todd.

1795—George Washington signs the Jay Treaty with Great Britain. Treaty of San Lorenzo, between U.S. and Spain, settles Florida boundary and gives U.S. right to navigate the Mississippi. James Polk is born near Pineville, North Carolina.

1796—Tennessee enters the Union. Washington gives his Farewell Address, refusing a third presidential term. John Adams is elected president and Thomas Jefferson vice-president.

1797—Adams recommends defense measures against possible war with France. Napoleon Bonaparte and his army march against Austrians in Italy. U.S. population is about 4,900,000.

1798—Washington is named commander-in-chief of the U.S. Army. Department of the Navy is created. Alien and Sedition Acts are passed. Napoleon's troops invade Egypt and Switzerland.

1799—George Washington dies at Mount Vernon, New York. James Monroe is elected governor of Virginia. French Revolution ends. Napoleon becomes ruler of France.

1800—Thomas Jefferson and Aaron Burr tie for president. U.S. capital is moved from Philadelphia to Washington, D.C. The White House is built as presidents' home. Spain returns Louisiana to France. Millard Fillmore is born in Locke, New York.

1801—After thirty-six ballots, House of Representatives elects Thomas Jefferson president, making Burr vice-president. James Madison is named secretary of state.

1802—Congress abolishes excise taxes. U.S. Military Academy is founded at West Point, New York.

1803—Ohio enters the Union. Louisiana Purchase treaty is signed with France, greatly expanding U.S. territory.

1804—Twelfth Amendment to the Constitution rules that president and vice-president be elected separately. Alexander Hamilton is killed by Vice-President Aaron Burr in a duel. Orleans Territory is established. Napoleon crowns himself emperor of France. Franklin Pierce is born in Hillsborough Lower Village, New Hampshire.

1805—Thomas Jefferson begins his second term as president. Lewis and Clark expedition reaches the Pacific Ocean.

1806—Coinage of silver dollars is stopped; resumes in 1836.

1807—Aaron Burr is acquitted in treason trial. Embargo Act closes U.S. ports to trade.

1808—James Madison is elected president. Congress outlaws importing slaves from Africa. Andrew Johnson is born in Raleigh, North Carolina.

1809—Abraham Lincoln is born near Hodgenville, Kentucky.

1810—U.S. population is 7,240,000.

1811—William Henry Harrison defeats Indians at Tippecanoe. Monroe is named secretary of state.

1812—Louisiana becomes a state. U.S. declares war on Britain (War of 1812). James Madison is reelected president. Napoleon invades Russia.

1813—British forces take Fort Niagara and Buffalo, New York.

1814—Francis Scott Key writes "The Star-Spangled Banner." British troops burn much of Washington, D.C., including the White House. Treaty of Ghent ends War of 1812. James Monroe becomes secretary of war.

1815—Napoleon meets his final defeat at Battle of Waterloo.

1816—James Monroe is elected president. Indiana becomes a state.

1817—Mississippi becomes a state. Construction on Erie Canal begins.

1818—Illinois enters the Union. The present thirteen-stripe flag is adopted. Border between U.S. and Canada is agreed upon.

1819—Alabama becomes a state. U.S. purchases Florida from Spain. Thomas Jefferson establishes the University of Virginia.

1820—James Monroe is reelected. In the Missouri Compromise, Maine enters the Union as a free (non-slave) state.

1821—Missouri enters the Union as a slave state. Santa Fe Trail opens the American Southwest. Mexico declares independence from Spain. Napoleon Bonaparte dies.

1822—U.S. recognizes Mexico and Colombia. Liberia in Africa is founded as a home for freed slaves. Ulysses S. Grant is born in Point Pleasant, Ohio. Rutherford B. Hayes is born in Delaware, Ohio.

1823—Monroe Doctrine closes North and South America to European colonizing or invasion.

1824—House of Representatives elects John Quincy Adams president when none of the four candidates wins a majority in national election. Mexico becomes a republic.

1825—Erie Canal is opened. U.S. population is 11,300,000.

1826—Thomas Jefferson and John Adams both die on July 4, the fiftieth anniversary of the Declaration of Independence.

1828—Andrew Jackson is elected president. Tariff of Abominations is passed, cutting imports.

1829—James Madison attends Virginia's constitutional convention. Slavery is abolished in Mexico. Chester A. Arthur is born in Fairfield, Vermont.

1830—Indian Removal Act to resettle Indians west of the Mississippi is approved.

1831—James Monroe dies in New York City. James A. Garfield is born in Orange, Ohio. Cyrus McCormick develops his reaper.

1832—Andrew Jackson, nominated by the new Democratic Party, is reelected president.

1833—Britain abolishes slavery in its colonies. Benjamin Harrison is born in North Bend, Ohio.

1835—Federal government becomes debt-free for the first time.

1836—Martin Van Buren becomes president. Texas wins independence from Mexico. Arkansas joins the Union. James Madison dies at Montpelier, Virginia.

1837—Michigan enters the Union. U.S. population is 15,900,000. Grover Cleveland is born in Caldwell, New Jersey.

1840—William Henry Harrison is elected president.

1841—President Harrison dies in Washington, D.C., one month after inauguration. Vice-President John Tyler succeeds him.

1843—William McKinley is born in Niles, Ohio.

1844—James Knox Polk is elected president. Samuel Morse sends first telegraphic message.

1845—Texas and Florida become states. Potato famine in Ireland causes massive emigration from Ireland to U.S. Andrew Jackson dies near Nashville, Tennessee.

1846—Iowa enters the Union. War with Mexico begins.

1847—U.S. captures Mexico City.

1848—John Quincy Adams dies in Washington, D.C. Zachary Taylor becomes president. Treaty of Guadalupe Hidalgo ends Mexico-U.S. war. Wisconsin becomes a state.

1849—James Polk dies in Nashville, Tennessee.

1850—President Taylor dies in Washington, D.C.; Vice-President Millard Fillmore succeeds him. California enters the Union, breaking tie between slave and free states.

1852—Franklin Pierce is elected president.

1853—Gadsden Purchase transfers Mexican territory to U.S.

1854—"War for Bleeding Kansas" is fought between slave and free states.

1855—Czar Nicholas I of Russia dies, succeeded by Alexander II.

1856—James Buchanan is elected president. In Massacre of Potawatomi Creek, Kansas-slavers are murdered by free-staters. Woodrow Wilson is born in Staunton, Virginia.

1857—William Howard Taft is born in Cincinnati, Ohio.

1858—Minnesota enters the Union. Theodore Roosevelt is born in New York City.

1859—Oregon becomes a state.

1860—Abraham Lincoln is elected president; South Carolina secedes from the Union in protest.

1861—Arkansas, Tennessee, North Carolina, and Virginia secede. Kansas enters the Union as a free state. Civil War begins.

1862—Union forces capture Fort Henry, Roanoke Island, Fort Donelson, Jacksonville, and New Orleans; Union armies are defeated at the battles of Bull Run and Fredericksburg. Martin Van Buren dies in Kinderhook, New York. John Tyler dies near Charles City, Virginia.

1863—Lincoln issues Emancipation Proclamation: all slaves held in rebelling territories are declared free. West Virginia becomes a state.

1864—Abraham Lincoln is reelected. Nevada becomes a state.

1865—Lincoln is assassinated in Washington, D.C., and succeeded by Andrew Johnson. U.S. Civil War ends on May 26. Thirteenth Amendment abolishes slavery. Warren G. Harding is born in Blooming Grove, Ohio.

1867—Nebraska becomes a state. U.S. buys Alaska from Russia for $7,200,000. Reconstruction Acts are passed.

1868—President Johnson is impeached for violating Tenure of Office Act, but is acquitted by Senate. Ulysses S. Grant is elected president. Fourteenth Amendment prohibits voting discrimination. James Buchanan dies in Lancaster, Pennsylvania.

1869—Franklin Pierce dies in Concord, New Hampshire.

1870—Fifteenth Amendment gives blacks the right to vote.

1872—Grant is reelected over Horace Greeley. General Amnesty Act pardons ex-Confederates. Calvin Coolidge is born in Plymouth Notch, Vermont.

1874—Millard Fillmore dies in Buffalo, New York. Herbert Hoover is born in West Branch, Iowa.

1875—Andrew Johnson dies in Carter's Station, Tennessee.

1876—Colorado enters the Union. "Custer's last stand": he and his men are massacred by Sioux Indians at Little Big Horn, Montana.

1877—Rutherford B. Hayes is elected president as all disputed votes are awarded to him.

1880—James A. Garfield is elected president.

1881—President Garfield is assassinated and dies in Elberon, New Jersey. Vice-President Chester A. Arthur succeeds him.

1882—U.S. bans Chinese immigration. Franklin D. Roosevelt is born in Hyde Park, New York.

1884—Grover Cleveland is elected president. Harry S. Truman is born in Lamar, Missouri.

1885—Ulysses S. Grant dies in Mount McGregor, New York.

1886—Statue of Liberty is dedicated. Chester A. Arthur dies in New York City.

1888—Benjamin Harrison is elected president.

1889—North Dakota, South Dakota, Washington, and Montana become states.

1890—Dwight D. Eisenhower is born in Denison, Texas. Idaho and Wyoming become states.

1892—Grover Cleveland is elected president.

1893—Rutherford B. Hayes dies in Fremont, Ohio.

1896—William McKinley is elected president. Utah becomes a state.

1898—U.S. declares war on Spain over Cuba.

1900—McKinley is reelected. Boxer Rebellion against foreigners in China begins.

1901—McKinley is assassinated by anarchist Leon Czolgosz in Buffalo, New York; Theodore Roosevelt becomes president. Benjamin Harrison dies in Indianapolis, Indiana.

1902—U.S. acquires perpetual control over Panama Canal.

1903—Alaskan frontier is settled.

1904—Russian-Japanese War breaks out. Theodore Roosevelt wins presidential election.

1905—Treaty of Portsmouth signed, ending Russian-Japanese War.

1906—U.S. troops occupy Cuba.

1907—President Roosevelt bars all Japanese immigration. Oklahoma enters the Union.

1908—William Howard Taft becomes president. Grover Cleveland dies in Princeton, New Jersey. Lyndon B. Johnson is born near Stonewall, Texas.

1909—NAACP is founded under W.E.B. DuBois

1910—China abolishes slavery.

1911—Chinese Revolution begins. Ronald Reagan is born in Tampico, Illinois.

1912—Woodrow Wilson is elected president. Arizona and New Mexico become states.

1913—Federal income tax is introduced in U.S. through the Sixteenth Amendment. Richard Nixon is born in Yorba Linda, California. Gerald Ford is born in Omaha, Nebraska.

1914—World War I begins.

1915—British liner *Lusitania* is sunk by German submarine.

1916—Wilson is reelected president.

1917—U.S. breaks diplomatic relations with Germany. Czar Nicholas of Russia abdicates as revolution begins. U.S. declares war on Austria-Hungary. John F. Kennedy is born in Brookline, Massachusetts.

1918—Wilson proclaims "Fourteen Points" as war aims. On November 11, armistice is signed between Allies and Germany.

1919—Eighteenth Amendment prohibits sale and manufacture of intoxicating liquors. Wilson presides over first League of Nations; wins Nobel Peace Prize. Theodore Roosevelt dies in Oyster Bay, New York.

1920—Nineteenth Amendment (women's suffrage) is passed. Warren Harding is elected president.

1921—Adolf Hitler's stormtroopers begin to terrorize political opponents.

1922—Irish Free State is established. Soviet states form USSR. Benito Mussolini forms Fascist government in Italy.

1923—President Harding dies in San Francisco, California; he is succeeded by Vice-President Calvin Coolidge.

1924—Coolidge is elected president. Woodrow Wilson dies in Washington, D.C. James Carter is born in Plains, Georgia. George Bush is born in Milton, Massachusetts.

1925—Hitler reorganizes Nazi Party and publishes first volume of *Mein Kampf.*

1926—Fascist youth organizations founded in Germany and Italy. Republic of Lebanon proclaimed.

1927—Stalin becomes Soviet dictator. Economic conference in Geneva attended by fifty-two nations.

1928—Herbert Hoover is elected president. U.S. and many other nations sign Kellogg-Briand pacts to outlaw war.

1929—Stock prices in New York crash on "Black Thursday"; the Great Depression begins.

1930—Bank of U.S. and its many branches close (most significant bank failure of the year). William Howard Taft dies in Washington, D.C.

1931—Emigration from U.S. exceeds immigration for first time as Depression deepens.

1932—Franklin D. Roosevelt wins presidential election in a Democratic landslide.

1933—First concentration camps are erected in Germany. U.S. recognizes USSR and resumes trade. Twenty-First Amendment repeals prohibition. Calvin Coolidge dies in Northampton, Massachusetts.

1934—Severe dust storms hit Plains states. President Roosevelt passes U.S. Social Security Act.

1936—Roosevelt is reelected. Spanish Civil War begins. Hitler and Mussolini form Rome-Berlin Axis.

1937—Roosevelt signs Neutrality Act.

1938—Roosevelt sends appeal to Hitler and Mussolini to settle European problems amicably.

1939—Germany takes over Czechoslovakia and invades Poland, starting World War II.

1940—Roosevelt is reelected for a third term.

1941—Japan bombs Pearl Harbor, U.S. declares war on Japan. Germany and Italy declare war on U.S.; U.S. then declares war on them.

1942—Allies agree not to make separate peace treaties with the enemies. U.S. government transfers more than 100,000 Nisei (Japanese-Americans) from west coast to inland concentration camps.

1943—Allied bombings of Germany begin.

1944—Roosevelt is reelected for a fourth term. Allied forces invade Normandy on D-Day.

1945—President Franklin D. Roosevelt dies in Warm Springs, Georgia; Vice-President Harry S. Truman succeeds him. Mussolini is killed; Hitler commits suicide. Germany surrenders. U.S. drops atomic bomb on Hiroshima; Japan surrenders: end of World War II.

1946—U.N. General Assembly holds its first session in London. Peace conference of twenty-one nations is held in Paris.

1947—Peace treaties are signed in Paris. "Cold War" is in full swing.

1948—U.S. passes Marshall Plan Act, providing $17 billion in aid for Europe. U.S. recognizes new nation of Israel. India and Pakistan become free of British rule. Truman is elected president.

1949—Republic of Eire is proclaimed in Dublin. Russia blocks land route access from Western Germany to Berlin; airlift begins. U.S., France, and Britain agree to merge their zones of occupation in West Germany. Apartheid program begins in South Africa.

1950—Riots in Johannesburg, South Africa, against apartheid. North Korea invades South Korea. U.N. forces land in South Korea and recapture Seoul.

1951—Twenty-Second Amendment limits president to two terms.

1952—Dwight D. Eisenhower resigns as supreme commander in Europe and is elected president.

1953—Stalin dies; struggle for power in Russia follows. Rosenbergs are executed for espionage.

1954—U.S. and Japan sign mutual defense agreement.

1955—Blacks in Montgomery, Alabama, boycott segregated bus lines.

1956—Eisenhower is reelected president. Soviet troops march into Hungary.

1957—U.S. agrees to withdraw ground forces from Japan. Russia launches first satellite, *Sputnik.*

1958—European Common Market comes into being. Fidel Castro begins war against Batista government in Cuba.

1959—Alaska becomes the forty-ninth state. Hawaii becomes fiftieth state. Castro becomes premier of Cuba. De Gaulle is proclaimed president of the Fifth Republic of France.

1960—Historic debates between Senator John F. Kennedy and Vice-President Richard Nixon are televised. Kennedy is elected president. Brezhnev becomes president of USSR.

1961—Berlin Wall is constructed. Kennedy and Khrushchev confer in Vienna. In Bay of Pigs incident, Cubans trained by CIA attempt to overthrow Castro.

1962—U.S. military council is established in South Vietnam.

1963—Riots and beatings by police and whites mark civil rights demonstrations in Birmingham, Alabama; 30,000 troops are called out, Martin Luther King, Jr., is arrested. Freedom marchers descend on Washington, D.C., to demonstrate. President Kennedy is assassinated in Dallas, Texas; Vice-President Lyndon B. Johnson is sworn in as president.

1964—U.S. aircraft bomb North Vietnam. Johnson is elected president. Herbert Hoover dies in New York City.

1965—U.S. combat troops arrive in South Vietnam.

1966—Thousands protest U.S. policy in Vietnam. National Guard quells race riots in Chicago.

1967—Six-Day War between Israel and Arab nations.

1968—Martin Luther King, Jr., is assassinated in Memphis, Tennessee. Senator Robert Kennedy is assassinated in Los Angeles. Riots and police brutality take place at Democratic National Convention in Chicago. Richard Nixon is elected president. Czechoslovakia is invaded by Soviet troops.

1969—Dwight D. Eisenhower dies in Washington, D.C. Hundreds of thousands of people in several U.S. cities demonstrate against Vietnam War.

1970—Four Vietnam War protesters are killed by National Guardsmen at Kent State University in Ohio.

1971—Twenty-Sixth Amendment allows eighteen-year-olds to vote.

1972—Nixon visits Communist China; is reelected president in near-record landslide. Watergate affair begins when five men are arrested in the Watergate hotel complex in Washington, D.C. Nixon announces resignations of aides Haldeman, Ehrlichman, and Dean and Attorney General Kleindienst as a result of Watergate-related charges. Harry S. Truman dies in Kansas City, Missouri.

1973—Vice-President Spiro Agnew resigns; Gerald Ford is named vice-president. Vietnam peace treaty is formally approved after nineteen months of negotiations. Lyndon B. Johnson dies in San Antonio, Texas.

1974—As a result of Watergate cover-up, impeachment is considered; Nixon resigns and Ford becomes president. Ford pardons Nixon and grants limited amnesty to Vietnam War draft evaders and military deserters.

1975—U.S. civilians are evacuated from Saigon, South Vietnam, as Communist forces complete takeover of South Vietnam.

1976—U.S. celebrates its Bicentennial. James Earl Carter becomes president.

1977—Carter pardons most Vietnam draft evaders, numbering some 10,000.

1980—Ronald Reagan is elected president.

1981—President Reagan is shot in the chest in assassination attempt. Sandra Day O'Connor is appointed first woman justice of the Supreme Court.

1983—U.S. troops invade island of Grenada.

1984—Reagan is reelected president. Democratic candidate Walter Mondale's running mate, Geraldine Ferraro, is the first woman selected for vice-president by a major U.S. political party.

1985—Soviet Communist Party secretary Konstantin Chernenko dies; Mikhail Gorbachev succeeds him. U.S. and Soviet officials discuss arms control in Geneva. Reagan and Gorbachev hold summit conference in Geneva. Racial tensions accelerate in South Africa.

1986—Space shuttle *Challenger* explodes shortly after takeoff; crew of seven dies. U.S. bombs bases in Libya. Corazon Aquino defeats Ferdinand Marcos in Philippine presidential election.

1987—Iraqi missile rips the U.S. frigate *Stark* in the Persian Gulf, killing thirty-seven American sailors. Congress holds hearings to investigate sale of U.S. arms to Iran to finance Nicaraguan *contra* movement.

1988—President Reagan and Soviet leader Gorbachev sign INF treaty, eliminating intermediate nuclear forces. Severe drought sweeps the United States. George Bush is elected president.

1989—East Germany opens Berlin Wall, allowing citizens free exit. Communists lose control of governments in Poland, Romania, and Czechoslovakia. Chinese troops massacre over 1,000 prodemocracy student demonstrators in Beijing's Tiananmen Square.

1990—Iraq annexes Kuwait, provoking the threat of war. East and West Germany are reunited. The Cold War between the United States and the Soviet Union comes to a close. Several Soviet republics make moves toward independence.

1991—Backed by a coalition of members of the United Nations, U.S. troops drive Iraqis from Kuwait. Latvia, Lithuania, and Estonia withdraw from the USSR. The Soviet Union dissolves as its republics secede to form a Commonwealth of Independent States.

1992—U.N. forces fail to stop fighting in territories of former Yugoslavia. More than fifty people are killed and more than six hundred buildings burned in rioting in Los Angeles. U.S. unemployment reaches eight-year high. Hurricane Andrew devastates southern Florida and parts of Louisiana. International relief supplies and troops are sent to combat famine and violence in Somalia.

1993—U.S.-led forces use airplanes and missiles to attack military targets in Iraq. William Jefferson Clinton becomes the forty-second U.S. president.

1994—Richard M. Nixon dies in New York City.

Index

Page numbers in boldface type indicate illustrations.

About the Author

Zachary Kent grew up in Little Falls, New Jersey, and received an English degree from St. Lawrence University. Following college he worked at a New York City literary agency for two years and then launched his writing career. To support himself while writing, he has worked as a taxi driver, a shipping clerk, and a house painter. Mr. Kent has had a lifelong interest in American history. Studying the U.S. presidents was his childhood hobby. His collection of presidential items includes books, pictures, and games, as well as several autographed letters.